God's Gifts to Me

A Prayer

Written by A. R. Pearson

Illustrated by Petra Marjanovics

Empowering Transformations   www.ltyvpublishing.co.uk

ISBN: 9781838283827

Book Cover Design: Listening To Your Voice Publishing
Illustrator: Petra Marjanovics
Editor: Annette Ruth Pearson
Typesetter: Annette Ruth Pearson
Proof-reader: Linda Green

Dedicated to

Safiyah-Nala and Skylar

Thank you for bringing such joy
into our lives.

I will praise You, for I am fearfully and wonderfully made.

Psalms 139:14 (NKJV)

This book belongs to

_____

God gave me eyes so I can see, His beauty all around.

God gave me ears so I can hear, mummy and daddy telling me, "I love you".

God gave me a nose so I can

smell the nice scent of flowers.

God gave me a tongue so I can taste, all of my favourite fruits and vegetables.

God gave me hands so I can

draw a beautiful picture for

my teacher.

God gave me arms so I can

hug my grandma or my

grandpa.

God gave me legs so I can run, jump and play, with all of my friends.

God gave me knees so I can kneel by my bed at the end of the day; to thank Him for all of the good things, He has given me.

Prayer

Thank you, God, for giving me
eyes to see.
Thank you, God, for giving me
ears to hear.
Thank you, God, for giving me
a nose to smell.
Thank you, God, for giving me
a tongue to taste.

Thank you, God, for giving me hands to draw.

Thank you, God, for giving me arms to hug.

Thank you, God, for giving me legs to run, jump and play.

Thank you, God, for giving me a great big heart to love my family.

MOST OF ALL

Thank you, God, for giving me

the best gift of all.

My heart, to love YOU.

Amen.

Notes to Parents, Carers or Teachers

Thank you so much for purchasing this book.

I hope you have been able to teach your young child or children how to be grateful for God's good gifts, given to them each day.

I hope you have been able to teach them how to pray simple prayers of thanksgiving.

I hope you have been able to show them in practical ways how they can be kind to others; by sharing gifts such as hugs, flowers, pictures and kind words.

I hope you had an opportunity to discuss the pictures and let them share their stories about their own day.

Record their ideas on the next two pages.

Prayers of Thanksgiving

I am grateful for ....

About the Author

Annette Ruth Pearson has worked in the education sector for over 30 years, as a teacher and school leader.

She had a passion for teaching children from a young age how to look after their mental health and wellbeing in practical ways.

As well as working in schools, she has been a volunteer in several organisations, empowering children, young people, their parents or carers to bring out their hidden greatness within.

In this her first children's book she looks at the topics of gratitude and prayer, and how they can become part of the daily lives of young children.

If you would like to learn more about the work Annette Ruth Pearson does, please email

info@ltyvpublishing.co.uk

If you have enjoyed reading this book, please remember to leave us a review.

Thank you

www.ingramcontent.com/pod-product-compliance
Lightning Source LLC
Chambersburg PA
CBHW041004170626
46815CB00002B/153